The Phœnician Virgins by Euripides

Euripides is rightly lauded as one of the great dramatists of all time. In his lifetime, he wrote over 90 plays and although only 18 have survived they reveal the scope and reach of his genius.

Euripides is identified with many theatrical innovations that have influenced drama all the way down to modern times, especially in the representation of traditional, mythical heroes as ordinary people in extraordinary circumstances.

As would be expected from a life lived 2,500 years ago, details of it are few and far between. Accounts of his life, written down the ages, do exist but whether much is reliable or surmised is open to debate.

Most accounts agree that he was born on Salamis Island around 480 BC, to mother Cleito and father Mnesarchus, a retailer who lived in a village near Athens. Upon the receipt of an oracle saying that his son was fated to win "crowns of victory", Mnesarchus insisted that the boy should train for a career in athletics.

However, what is clear is that athletics was not to be the way to win crowns of victory. Euripides had been lucky enough to have been born in the era as the other two masters of Greek Tragedy; Sophocles and Æschylus. It was in their footsteps that he was destined to follow.

His first play was performed some thirteen years after the first of Socrates plays and a mere three years after Æschylus had written his classic The Oristria.

Theatre was becoming a very important part of the Greek culture. The Dionysia, held annually, was the most important festival of theatre and second only to the fore-runner of the Olympic games, the Panathenia, held every four years, in appeal.

Euripides first competed in the City Dionysia, in 455 BC, one year after the death of Æschylus, and, incredibly, it was not until 441 BC that he won first prize. His final competition in Athens was in 408 BC. The Bacchae and Iphigenia in Aulis were performed after his death in 405 BC and first prize was awarded posthumously. Altogether his plays won first prize only five times.

Euripides was also a great lyric poet. In Medea, for example, he composed for his city, Athens, "the noblest of her songs of praise". His lyric skills however are not just confined to individual poems: "A play of Euripides is a musical whole....one song echoes motifs from the preceding song, while introducing new ones."

Much of his life and his whole career coincided with the struggle between Athens and Sparta for hegemony in Greece but he didn't live to see the final defeat of his city.

Euripides fell out of favour with his fellow Athenian citizens and retired to the court of Archelaus, king of Macedon, who treated him with consideration and affection.

At his death, in around 406BC, he was mourned by the king, who, refusing the request of the Athenians that his remains be carried back to the Greek city, buried him with much splendor within his own dominions. His tomb was placed at the confluence of two streams, near Arethusa in Macedonia, and a cenotaph was built to his memory on the road from Athens towards the Piraeus.

Index of Contents

THE PERSONS

JOCASTA.
TUTOR.
ANTIGONE.
CHORUS OF PHŒNICIAN VIRGINS.
POLYNICES.
ETEOCLES.
CREON.
MENŒCEUS.
TIRECIAS.
MESSENGERS.
ŒDIPUS.

SCENE

In the Court before the royal palace at Thebes.

THE ARGUMENT

Eteocles having gotten possession of the throne of Thebes, deprived his brother Polynices of his share; but he having come as an exile to Argos, married the daughter of the king Adrastus; but ambitious of returning to his country, and having persuaded his father-in-law, he assembled a great army for Thebes against his brother. His mother Jocasta made him come into the city, under sanction of a truce, and first confer with his brother respecting the empire. But Eteocles being violent and fierce from having possessed the empire, Jocasta could not reconcile her children.— Polynices, prepared as against an enemy, rushed out of the city. Now Tiresias prophesied that victory should be on the side of the Thebans, if Menœceus the son of Creon would give himself up to be sacrificed to Mars. Creon refused to give his son to the city, but the youth was willing, and, his father pointing out to him the means of flight and giving him money, he put himself to death.—The Thebans slew the leaders of the Argives. Eteocles and Polynices in a single combat slew each other, and their mother having found the corses of her sons laid violent hands on herself; and Creon her brother received the kingdom. The Argives defeated in battle retired. But Creon, being morose, would not give up those of the enemy who had fallen at Thebes, for sepulture, and exposed the body of Polynices without burial, and banished Œdipus from his country; in the one instance disregarding the laws of humanity, in the other giving way to passion, nor feeling pity for him after his calamity.

JOCASTA

O thou that cuttest thy path through the constellations of heaven, and art mounted on thy golden-joined seats, thou sun, whirling thy flame with thy swift steeds, how inauspicious didst thou dart thy ray on that day when Cadmus came to this land having left the sea-washed coast of Phœnicia; who in former time having married Harmonia, daughter of Venus, begat Polydorus; from him they say sprung Labdacus, and from him Laius. But I am the daughter of Menœceus, and Creon my brother was born of the same mother; me they call Jocasta (for this name my father gave me), and Laius takes me for his wife; but after that he was childless, for a long time sharing my bed in the palace, he went and inquired of Apollo, and at the same time demands the mutual offspring of male children in his family; but the God said, "O king of Thebes renowned for its chariots, sow not for such a harvest of children against the will of the Gods, for if thou shalt beget a son, he that is born shall slay thee, and the whole of thy house shall wade through blood." But having yielded to pleasure, and having fallen into inebriety, he begot to us a son, and having begot him, feeling conscious of his error and the command of the God, gives the babe to some herdsmen to expose at the meads of Juno and the rock of Cithæron, having bored sharp-pointed iron through the middle of his ankles, from which circumstance Greece gave him the name of Œdipus. But him the grooms who attend the steeds of Polybus find and carry home, and placed him in the arms of their mistress. But she rested beneath her bosom him that gave me a mother's pangs, and persuades her husband that she had brought forth. But now my son showing signs of manhood in his darkening cheek, either having suspected it by instinct, or having learned it from some one, went to the temple of Apollo, desirous of discovering his parents; at the same time went Laius my husband, seeking to gain intelligence of his son who had been exposed, if he were no longer living; and both met at the same point of the road at Phocis where it divides itself; and the charioteer of Laius commands him, "Stranger, withdraw out of the way of princes;" but he moved slowly, in silence, with haughty spirit; but the steeds with their hoof dyed with blood the tendons of his feet. At this (but why need I relate each horrid circumstance besides the deed itself?) the son kills his father, and having taken the chariot, sends it as a present to his foster-father Polybus. Now at this time the sphinx preyed vulture-like upon the city with rapacity, my husband now no more, Creon my brother proclaims that he will give my bed as a reward to him who would solve the enigma of the crafty virgin. But by some chance or other Œdipus my son happens to discover the riddle of the sphinx, and he receives as a prize the sceptre of this land, and marries me, his mother, wretched he not knowing it, nor knew his mother that she was lying down with her son. And I bear children to my child, two sons, Eteocles and the illustrious Polynices, and two daughters, one her father named Ismene, the elder I called Antigone. But Œdipus, after having gone through all sufferings, having discovered in my bed the marriage with his mother, he perpetrated a deed of horror on his own eyes, having drenched in blood their pupils with his golden buckles. But after that the cheek of my children grows dark with manly down, they hid their father confined with bolts that his sad fortune might be forgotten, which indeed required the greatest policy. He is still living in the palace, but sick in mind through his misfortunes he imprecates the most unhallowed curses on his children, that they may share this house with the sharpened sword. But these two, dreading lest the Gods should bring to completion these curses, should they dwell together, in friendly compact determined that Polynices the younger son should first go a willing exile from this land, but that Eteocles remaining here should hold the sceptre for a year, changing in his turn; but after that he sat on the throne of power, he moves not from his seat, but drives Polynices an exile from this land. But he having fled to Argos, and having contracted an alliance with Adrastus, assembles together and leads a vast army of Argives; and having marched to these very walls with seven gates he demands his father's sceptre and his share of the land. But I to quell this strife persuaded my son to come to his brother, confiding in a truce before he grasped the spear. And the messenger who was sent declares that he will come. But, O thou that inhabitest the shining clouds of heaven, Jove, preserve us, give reconciliation to my children; it becomes thee, if thou art wise, not to suffer the same man always to be unfortunate.

TUTOR, ANTIGONE.

TUTOR
O thou fair bud in thy father's house, Antigone, since thy mother has permitted thee to leave the virgin's apartments for the extreme chamber of the mansion, in order to view the Argive army in compliance with thy entreaties, yet stay, until I shall first investigate the path, lest any citizen should appear in the pass, and to me taunts should come as a slave, and to thee as a princess: and I who well know each circumstance will tell you all that I saw or heard from the Argives, when I went bearing the offer of a truce to thy brother, from this place thither, and again to this place from him. But no citizen approaches this house; come, ascend with thy steps these ancient stairs of cedar, and survey the plains, and by the streams of Ismenus and Dirce's fount how great is the host of the enemy.

ANTIGONE
Stretch forth now, stretch forth thine aged hand from the stairs to my youth, raising up the steps of my feet.

TUTOR
Behold, join thy hand, virgin, thou hast come in lucky hour, for the Pelasgian host is now in motion, and they are separating the bands from one another.

ANTIGONE
O awful daughter of Latona, Hecate, the field all brass gleaming like lightning.

TUTOR
For Polynices hath not come tamely to this land, raging with host of horsemen, and ten thousand shields.

ANTIGONE
Are the gates fastened with bars, and is the brazen bolt fitted to the stone-work of Amphion's wall?

TUTOR
Take courage; as to the interior the city is safe, But view the first chief, if thou desirest to know.

ANTIGONE
Who is he with the white-plumed helmet, who commands in the van of the army, moving lightly round on his arm his brazen shield?

TUTOR
He is a leader, lady.

ANTIGONE
Who is he? From whom sprung? Speak, aged man, what is he called by name?

TUTOR

He indeed is called by birth a Mycenæan, and he dwells at the streams of Lerna, the king Hippomedon.

ANTIGONE
Ah! how haughty, how terrible to behold! like to an earth-born giant, starlike in countenance amidst his painted devices, he corresponds not with the race of mortals.

TUTOR
Dost thou not see him now passing the stream of Dirce, a general?

ANTIGONE
Here is another, another fashion of arms. But who is he?

TUTOR
He is the son of Œneus, Tydeus, and bears on his breast the Ætolian Mars.

ANTIGONE
Is this the prince, O aged man, who is husband to the sister of my brother's wife? In his arms how different of color, of barbaric mixture!

TUTOR
For all the Ætolians, my child, bear the target, and hurl with the lance, most certain in their aim.

ANTIGONE
But how, O aged man, dost thou know these things so perfectly?

TUTOR
Having seen the devices of the shields, then I remarked them, when I went to bear the offer of a truce to thy brother, beholding which, I recognize the warriors.

ANTIGONE
But who is this, who is passing round the tomb of Zethus, with clustering locks, in his eyes a Gorgon to behold, in appearance a youth?

TUTOR
A general he is.

ANTIGONE
How a crowd in complete armor attends him behind!

TUTOR
This is Parthenopæus, son of Atalanta.

ANTIGONE
But, may Diana who rushes over the mountains with his mother destroy him, having subdued him with her arrows, who has come against my city to destroy it.

TUTOR
May it be so, my child, nevertheless they are come with justice to this land; wherefore also I fear lest the Gods should judge rightly.

ANTIGONE

Where, but where is he who was born of one mother with me in hard fate, O dearest old man; tell me, where is Polynices?

TUTOR

He is standing near the tomb of the seven virgin daughters of Niobe, close by Adrastus. Seest thou him?

ANTIGONE

I see indeed, but not distinctly; but somehow I see the resemblance of his form, and his shape shadowed out. Would that with my feet I could perform the journey of the winged cloud through the air to my brother, then would I fling my arms round his dearest neck, after so long a time a wretched exile. How splendid is he, O old man, in his golden armor, glittering like the morning rays of the sun.

TUTOR

He will come to this house confiding in the truce, so as to fill thee with joy.

ANTIGONE

But who, O aged man, is this, who guides his milk-white steeds seated in his chariot?

TUTOR

The prophet Amphiaraus this, O my mistress, and with him the victims, the libations of the earth delighting in blood.

ANTIGONE

O thou daughter of the brightly girded sun, thou moon, golden-circled light, applying what quiet and temperate blows to his steeds does he direct his chariot! But where is he who utters such dreadful insults against this city, Capaneus?

TUTOR

He is scanning the approach to the towers, measuring the walls both from their foundation to the top.

ANTIGONE

O vengeance, and ye loud-roaring thunders of Jove, and thou blasting fire of the lightning, do thou quell this more-than-mortal arrogance. This is he who will with his spear give to Mycenæ, and to the streams of Lernæan Triæna, and to the Amymonian waters of Neptune, the Theban women, having invested them with slavery. Sever, O awful Goddess, never, O daughter of Jove, with golden clusters of ringlets, Diana, may I endure servitude.

TUTOR

My child, enter the palace, and at home remain in thy virgin chambers, since thou hast arrived at the indulgement of thy desire, as to what you were anxious to behold. For, since confusion has entered the city, a crowd of women is advancing to the royal palace. The race of women is prone to complaint, and if they find but small occasion for words, they add more, and it is a sort of pleasure to women, to speak nothing well-advised one of another.

CHORUS

I have come, having left the Tyrian wave, the first-fruits of Loxias, from the sea-washed Phœnicia, a slave for the shrine of Apollo, that I might dwell under the snowy brows of Parnassus, having sped my way over the Ionian flood by the oar, the west wind with its blasts riding over the barren plains of waters which flow round Sicily, the sweetest murmur in the heavens. Chosen out from my city the fairest present to Apollo, I came to the land of the Cadmeans, the illustrious descendants of Agenor, sent hither to these kindred towers of Laius. And I am made the slave of Apollo in like manner with the golden-framed images. Moreover the water of Castalia awaits me, to lave the virgin pride of my tresses, in the ministry of Apollo. O blazing rock, the flame of fire that seems double above the Dionysian heights of Bacchus, and thou vine, who distillest the daily nectar, producing the fruitful cluster from the tender shoot; and ye divine caves of the dragon, and ye mountain watch-towers of the Gods, and thou hallowed snowy mountain, would that I were the chorus of the immortal God free from alarms encompassing thee around, by the caves of Apollo in the centre of the earth, having left Dirce. But now impetuous Mars having advanced before the walls lights up against this city, which may the Gods avert, hostile war; for common are the misfortunes of friends, and common is it, if this land defended by its seven turrets should suffer any calamity, to the Phœnician country, alas! alas! common is the affinity, common are the descendants of Io bearing horns; of which woes I have a share. But a thick cloud of shields glares around the city, the likeness of gory battle, bearing which destruction from the Furies to the children of Œdipus Mars shall quickly advance. O Pelasgian Argos, I dread thy power, and vengeance from the Gods, for he rushes not his arms to this war unjustly, who seeks to recover his home.

POLYNICES, CHORUS.

POLYNICES
The bolts indeed of the gate-keepers have with ease admitted me, that I might come within the walls; wherefore also I fear, lest, having caught me within their nets, they let not my body go without bloodshed. On which account my eye must be turned about on every side, both that way and this, lest there be treachery. But armed in my hand with this sword, I will give myself confidence of daring. Ha! Who is this; or do we fear a noise? Every thing appears terrible even to the bold, when his foot shall pass across a hostile country. I trust however in my mother, at the same time I scarce trust, who persuaded me to come hither confiding in a truce. But protection is nigh; for the hearths of the altars are at hand, and houses not deserted. Come. I will let go my sword into its dark scabbard, and will question these who they are, that are standing at the palace. Ye female strangers, tell me, from what country do ye approach Grecian habitations?

CHORUS
The Phœnician is my paternal country, she that nurtured me: and the descendants of Agenor sent me hither from the spoils, the first-fruits to Apollo. And while the renowned son of Œdipus was preparing to send me to the revered shrine, and to the altars of Phœbus, in the mean time the Argives marched against the city. But do thou in turn answer me, who thou art, who hast come to this bulwark of the Theban land with its seven gates?

POLYNICES
My father is Œdipus the son of Laius; Jocasta daughter of Menœceus brought me forth; the Theban people call me Polynices.

CHORUS
O thou allied to the sons of Agenor, my lords, by whom I was sent, I fall at thy knees in lowly posture, O king, preserving my country's custom. Thou hast come, thou hast come, after a length of time, to thy paternal land. O venerable matron, come forth quickly, open the doors; dost thou hear, O mother, that producedst this hero? why dost thou delay to leave thy lofty mansion, and to embrace thy child with thine arms?

JOCASTA, POLYNICES, CHORUS.

JOCASTA

Hearing the Phœnician tongue, ye virgins, within this mansion, I drag my steps trembling with age. Ah! my son, after length of time, after numberless days, I behold thy countenance; clasp thy mother's bosom in thine arms, throw around her thy kisses, and the dark ringlets of thy clustering hair, shading my neck. Ah! scarce possible is it that thou appearest in thy mother's arms so unhoped for, and so unexpected. How shall I address thee? how shall I perform all? how shall I, walking in rapture around thee on that side and this, both with my hands and words, reap the varied pleasure, the delight of my former joys? O my son, thou hast left thy father's house deserted, sent away an exile by wrongful treatment from thy brother. How longed for by thy friends! how longed for by Thebes! From which time I am both shorn of my hoary locks, letting them fall with tears, with wailing; deprived, my child, of the white robes, I receive in exchange around me these dark and dismal weeds. But the old man in the palace deprived of sight, always preserving with tears regret for the unanimity of the brothers which is separated from the family, has madly rushed on self-destruction with the sword and with the noose above the beams of the house, bewailing the curse imprecated on his children; and with cries of woe he is always hidden in darkness. But thou, my child, I hear, art both joined in marriage, and hast the joys of love in a foreign family, and cherishest a foreign alliance; intolerable to this thy mother and to the aged Laius, the woe of a foreign marriage brought upon us. But neither did I light the torch of fire for you, as is customary in the marriage rites, as befits the happy mother; nor was Ismenus careful of the bridal rites in the luxury of the bath: and the entrance of thy bride was made in silence through the Theban city. May these ills perish, whether the sword, or discord, or thy father is the cause, or whether fate has rushed with violence upon the house of Œdipus; for the weight of these sorrows has fallen upon me.

CHORUS

Parturition with the attendant throes has a wonderful effect on women; and somehow the whole race of women have strong affection toward their children.

POLYNICES

My mother, determining wisely, and yet not determining wisely, have I come to men my foes; but it is necessary that all must be enamored of their country; but whoever says otherwise, pleases himself with vain words, but has his heart there. But so far have I come to trouble and terror, lest any treachery from my brother should slay me, so that having my hand on my sword I proceeded through the city rolling round my eye; but one thing is on my side, the truce and thy faith, which has brought me within my paternal walls: but I have come with many tears, after a length of time beholding the courts and the altars of the Gods, and the schools wherein I was brought up, and the fount of Dirce, from which banished by injustice, I inhabit a foreign city, having a stream of tears flowing through my eyes. But, for from one woe springs a second, I behold thee having thy head shorn of its locks, and these sable garments; alas me! on account of my misfortunes. How dreadful a thing, mother, is the enmity of relations, having means of reconciliation seldom to be brought about! For how fares the old man my father in the palace, vainly looking upon darkness; and how fare my two sisters? Are they indeed bewailing my wretched banishment?

JOCASTA

Some God miserably destroys the race of Œdipus; for thus began it, when I brought forth children in that unhallowed manner, and thy father married me in evil hour, and thou didst spring forth. But why relate these things? What is sent by the Gods we must bear. But how I may ask the questions I wish, I know not, for I fear lest I wound at all thy feelings; but I have a great desire.

POLYNICES

But inquire freely, leave nothing out. For what you wish, my mother, this is dear to me.

JOCASTA
I ask thee therefore, first, for the information that I wish to obtain. What is the being deprived of one's country, is it a great ill?

POLYNICES
The greatest: and greater is it in deed than in word.

JOCASTA
What is the reason of that? What is that so harsh to exiles?

POLYNICES
One thing, and that the greatest, not to have the liberty of speaking.

JOCASTA
This that you have mentioned belongs to a slave, not to give utterance to what one thinks.

POLYNICES
It is necessary to bear with the follies of those in power.

JOCASTA
And this is painful, to be unwise with the unwise.

POLYNICES
But for interest we must bend to slavery contrary to our nature.

JOCASTA
But hopes support exiles, as report goes.

POLYNICES
They look upon them with favorable eyes, at least, but are slow of foot.

JOCASTA
Hath not time shown them to be vain?

POLYNICES
They have a certain sweet delight to set against misfortunes.

JOCASTA
But whence wert thou supported, before thou foundest means of sustenance by thy marriage?

POLYNICES
At one time I had food for the day, at another I had not.

JOCASTA
And did the friends and hosts of your father not assist you?

POLYNICES
Be prosperous, and thou shalt have friends: but friends are none, should one be in adversity.

JOCASTA
Did not thy noble birth raise thee to great distinction?

POLYNICES
To want is wretched; high birth fed me not.

JOCASTA
Their own country, it appears, is the dearest thing to men.

POLYNICES
You can not express by words how dear it is.

JOCASTA
But how camest thou to Argos? What intention hadst thou?

POLYNICES
Apollo gave a certain oracle to Adrastus.

JOCASTA
What is this thou hast mentioned? I am unable to discover.

POLYNICES
To unite his daughters in marriage with a boar and lion.

JOCASTA
And what part of the name of beasts belongs to you, my son.

POLYNICES
I know not. The God called me to this fortune.

JOCASTA
For the God is wise. But in what manner didst thou obtain her bed?

POLYNICES
It was night; but I came to the portals of Adrastus.

JOCASTA
In search of a couch to rest on, as a wandering exile?

POLYNICES
This was the case, and then indeed there came a second exile.

JOCASTA
Who was this? how unfortunate then was he also!

POLYNICES
Tydeus, who they say sprung from Œneus his sire.

JOCASTA
In what then did Adrastus liken you to beasts?

POLYNICES
Because we came to blows for lodging.

JOCASTA
In this the son of Talaus understood the oracle.

POLYNICES
And gave in marriage to us two his two virgin daughters.

JOCASTA
Art thou fortunate then in thy marriage alliance, or unfortunate?

POLYNICES
My marriage can not be found fault with up to this day.

JOCASTA
But how didst thou persuade an army to follow you hither?

POLYNICES
Adrastus swore this oath to his two sons-in-law, that he would replace both in their own country, but me first. And many princes of the Argives and Mycenæans are at hand, rendering to me a sad, but necessary favor; for I am leading an army against this my own city; but I have called the Gods to witness how unwillingly I have raised the spear against my dearest parents. But the dissolution of these ills extends to thee, my mother, that having reconciled the friendly brothers, you may free from toil me and thyself, and the whole city. It is a proverb long ago chanted, but nevertheless I will repeat it; wealth is honored most of all things by men, and has the greatest influence of any thing among men. In pursuit of which I am come, leading hither ten thousand spears: for a nobly-born man in poverty is nothing.

CHORUS
And see Eteocles here comes to this mediation; thy business it is, O Jocasta, being their mother, to speak words, with which thou shalt reconcile thy children.

ETEOCLES, POLYNICES, JOCASTA, CHORUS.

ETEOCLES
Mother, I am present; giving this grace to thee, I have come; what must I do? Let some one begin the conference. Since arranging also around the walls the chariots of the bands, I restrained the city, that I may hear from thee the common terms of reconciliation, for which thou hast permitted this man to come within the walls under sanction of a truce, having persuaded me.

JOCASTA
Stay; precipitate haste has not justice; but slow counsels perform most deeds in wisdom. But repress that fierce eye and those blasts of rage; for thou art not looking on the Gorgon's head cut off at the neck, but thou art looking on thy brother who is come to thee. And do thou again, Polynices, turn thy face toward thy brother; for looking at the same point with thine eyes, thou wilt both speak better, and receive his words better. But I wish to give you a wise piece of advice. When a friend is enraged with a man his friend, having met him face to face, let him fix his eyes on his friend's eyes, this only ought he to consider, the end for which he is come, but to have no recollection of former grievances. Thy words then first, my son, Polynices; for thou art come leading an army of Argives,

having suffered injustice, as thou sayest; and may some God be umpire and the reconciler of your strife.

POLYNICES
The speech of truth is simple, and those things which are just need not wily interpretations; for they have energy themselves; but the unjust speech, unsound in itself, requires cunning preparations to gloze it. But I have previously considered for my father's house, and my own advantage and that of this man; desiring to escape the curses, which Œdipus denounced formerly against us, I myself of my own accord departed from this land, having given him to rule over his own country for the space of a year, so that I myself should have the government again, having received it in turn, and not having come into enmity and bloodshed with this man to perform some evil deed, and to suffer what is now taking place. But he having assented to this, and having brought the Gods to witness his oaths, has performed nothing of what he promised, but himself holds the regal power and my share of the palace. And now I am ready, having received my own right, to send the army away from out of this land, and to regulate my house, having received it in my turn, and to give it up again to this man for the same space of time, and neither to lay my country waste, nor to apply to its towers the means of ascent by the firmly-fixed ladders. Which, should I not meet with justice, will I endeavor to put in execution: and I call the Gods as witnesses of this, that acting in every thing with justice, I am without justice deprived of my country in the most unrighteous manner. These individual circumstances, mother, not having collected together intricacies of argument, have I declared, but both to the wise and to the illiterate just, as appears to me.

CHORUS
To me indeed, although we have not been brought up according to the Grecian land, nevertheless to me thou appearest to speak with judgment.

ETEOCLES
If the same thing were judged honorable alike by all, and at the same time wise, there would not be doubtful strife among men. But now nothing is similar, nothing the same among mortals, except in names; but the sense is not the same, for I, my mother, will speak having kept nothing back; I would mount to the rising of the stars, and sink beneath the earth, were I able to perform this, so that I might possess the greatest of the Goddesses, kingly power. This prize then, my mother, I am not willing rather to give up to another, than to preserve for myself. For it implies cowardice in him, whoever having lost the greater share, hath received the less; but in addition to this I feel ashamed, that this man having come with arms, and laying the country waste, should obtain what he wishes; for to Thebes this would be a reproach, if through fear of the Mycenæan spear I should give up my sceptre for this man to hold. But he ought, my mother, to effect a reconciliation, not by arms: for speech does every thing which even the sword of the enemy could do. But if he is desirous of inhabiting this land in any other way, it is in his power; but the other point I will never give up willingly. When it is in my power to rule, ever to be a slave to him? Wherefore come fire, come sword, yoke thy steeds, fill the plains with chariots, since I will not give up my kingly power to this man. For if one must be unjust, it is most glorious to be unjust concerning empire, but in every thing else one should be just.

CHORUS
It is not right to speak well, where the deeds are not glorious; for this is not honorable, but galling to justice.

JOCASTA
My son, Eteocles, not every ill is added to age, but experience has it in its power to evince more wisdom than youth. Why, my child, dost thou so desirously court ambition, the most baneful of the

deities? do not thou; the Goddess is unjust. But she hath entered into many families and happy states and hath come forth again, to the destruction of those who have to do with her. Of whom thou art madly enamored. This is more noble, my son, to honor equality, which ever links friends with friends, and states with states, and allies with allies: for equality is sanctioned by law among men. But the lesser share is ever at enmity with the greater, and straight begins the day of hatred. For equality arranged also among mortals measures, and the divisions of weights, and defined numbers. And the dark eye of night, and the light of the sun, equally walk their annual round, and neither of them being overcome hath envy of the other. Thus the sun and the night are subservient to men, but wilt not thou brook having an equal share of government, and give his share to him? Then where is justice? Why dost thou honor so unboundedly that prosperous injustice, royalty, and think so highly of her? Is the being conspicuous honorable? At least, it is empty honor. Or dost thou desire to labor much, possessing much in thy house? but what is superfluity? It possesses but a name; since a sufficiency indeed to the temperate is abundance. Neither do men enjoy riches as their own, but having the property of the Gods do we cherish them. And when they list, again do they take them away. Come, if I ask thee, having proposed together two measures, whether it is thy wish to reign, or save the city? Wilt thou say, to reign? But should he conquer thee, and the Argive spears overcome the Cadmæan forces, thou wilt behold this city of the Thebans vanquished, thou wilt behold many captive maidens with violence ravished by men your foes. Bitter then to Thebes will be the power which thou seekest to hold; but yet thou art ambitious of it. To thee I say this: but to thee, Polynices, say I, that Adrastus hath conferred an unwise favor on thee; and foolishly hast thou also come to destroy this city. Come, if thou wilt subdue this land (may which never happen), by the Gods, how wilt thou erect trophies of thy spear? And how again wilt thou sacrifice the first-fruits, having conquered thy country? and how wilt thou engrave upon the spoils by the waters of Inachus, "Having laid Thebes in ashes, Polynices consecrated these shields to the Gods?" Never, my son, may it come to thee to receive such glory from the Greeks. But again, shouldest thou be conquered, and should the arms of the other prevail, how wilt thou return to Argos having left behind ten thousand dead? Surely some one will say, O! unfortunate marriage alliance! O Adrastus, who placed them on us, through the nuptials of one bride we are lost! Thou art hastening two ills, my son, to be deprived of those, and to fail in this. Give up your too great ardor, give it up; the follies of two when they clash together in the same point, are the most hateful ill.

CHORUS

O ye Gods, may ye be averters of these ills, and grant to the children of Œdipus some means of agreement.

ETEOCLES

My mother, this is not a contest of words, but intervening time is fruitlessly wasted; and thy earnestness avails nothing; for we shall not agree in any other way, than on the terms proposed, that I holding the sceptre be monarch of this land. Forbearing then tedious admonitions, let me have my way; and do thou begone from out these walls, or thou shalt die.

POLYNICES

By whose hand? Who is there so invulnerable, who having pointed the murderous sword against me, shall not bear the same fate?

ETEOCLES

He is near, not far removed from thee: dost thou look on these my hands?

POLYNICES

I see them. But wealth is cowardly, and feeble, loving life.

ETEOCLES

And therefore hast thou come, with such a host against one who is nothing in arms?

POLYNICES

For a cautious general is better than one daring.

ETEOCLES

Thou art insolent, having trusted in the truce, which preserves you from death.

POLYNICES

A second time again I demand of you the sceptre and my share of the land.

ETEOCLES

I will admit no demand, for I will regulate my own family.

POLYNICES

Holding more than your share?

ETEOCLES

I own it; but quit this land.

POLYNICES

O ye altars of my paternal Gods.

ETEOCLES

Which thou art come to destroy?

POLYNICES

Do ye hear me?

ETEOCLES

Who will hear thee, who art marching against thy country?

POLYNICES

And ye shrines of the Gods delighting in the milk-white steeds;

ETEOCLES

Who hate thee.

POLYNICES

I am driven out of my own country.

ETEOCLES

For thou hast come to destroy it.

POLYNICES

With injustice indeed, O ye Gods!

ETEOCLES

At Mycenæ call upon the Gods, not here.

POLYNICES
Thou art impious.

ETEOCLES
But not my country's enemy, as thou art.

POLYNICES
Who drives me out without my share.

ETEOCLES
And I will put thee to death in addition.

POLYNICES
My father, hearest thou what I suffer?

ETEOCLES
For he hears what wrongs thou doest.

POLYNICES
And thou, my mother?

ETEOCLES
It is not lawful for thee to mention thy mother.

POLYNICES
O my city!

ETEOCLES
To Argos go, and call on Lerna's stream.

POLYNICES
I will go, do not distress thyself; but thee, my mother, I mention with honor.

ETEOCLES
Depart from out of the country.

POLYNICES
I will go out; but grant me to see my father.

ETEOCLES
You will not obtain your request.

POLYNICES
But my virgin sisters then.

ETEOCLES
Never shalt thou behold these.

POLYNICES
O my sisters!

ETEOCLES
Why callest thou on these—being their greatest enemy?

POLYNICES
My mother, but thou farewell.

JOCASTA
Do I experience any thing that is well, my son?

POLYNICES
I am no longer thy child.

JOCASTA
To many troubles was I born.

POLYNICES
For he throws insults on us.

ETEOCLES
For I am insulted in turn.

POLYNICES
Where wilt thou stand before the towers?

ETEOCLES
Why dost thou ask me this question?

POLYNICES
I will oppose myself to thee, to slay thee.

ETEOCLES
Desire of this seizes me also.

JOCASTA
Wretched me! what will ye do, my children?

POLYNICES
The deed itself will show.

JOCASTA
Will ye not escape your father's curses?

ETEOCLES
Let the whole house perish!

POLYNICES
Since soon my blood-stained sword will not remain any longer in inactivity. But I call to witness the land that nurtured me, and the Gods, how dishonored I am driven from this land, suffering such foul treatment, as a slave and not born of the same father Œdipus. And if any thing befalls thee, my city, blame not me, but him; for against my will have I come, and against my will am I driven from this land. And thou, king Apollo, God of our streets, and ye shrines, farewell, and ye my equals, and ye

altars of the Gods receiving the victims; for I know not if it is allowed me ever again to address you. But hope does not yet slumber, in which I have trusted with the favor of the Gods, that having slain this man, I shall be master of this Theban land.

ETEOCLES
Depart from out of the country; with truth indeed did your father give you the name of Polynices by some divine foreknowledge, a name corresponding with strife.

CHORUS
Cadmus came from Tyre to this land, before whom the quadrupede heifer bent with willing fall, showing the accomplishment of the oracle, where the divine word ordered him to colonize the plains of the Aonians productive of wheat, where indeed the fair-flowing stream of the water of Dirce passes over the verdant and deep-furrowed fields, where Semele produced Bacchus, by her marriage with Jove, whom the wreathed ivy twining around him instantly, while yet a babe, blest and covered with its verdant shady branches, an event to be celebrated with Bacchic revel by the Theban virgins and inspired women. There was the bloodstained dragon of Mars, the savage guard, watching with far-rolling eyeballs over the flowing fountains and grassy streams; whom Cadmus, having come for water for purification, slew with a fragment of rock, the destroyer of the monster having thrown his arms with blows on his blood-stained head, by the counsel of the divine Pallas born without mother, having thrown the teeth fallen to the earth upon the deep-furrowed plains. Whence the earth sent forth a spectacle, an armed host above the extreme limits of the ground; but iron-hearted slaughter again united them with their beloved earth; and sprinkled with blood the ground which showed them to the serene gales of the air. And thee, sprung of old from our ancestor Io, Epaphus, O progeny of Jove, on thee have I called, have I called in a foreign tongue, with prayers in foreign accent, come, come to this land (thy descendants have founded it), where the two Goddesses Proserpine and the dear Goddess Ceres, queen of all (since earth nurtures all things), have held their possessions, send the fire-bearing Goddesses to defend this land: since every thing is easy to the Gods.

ETEOCLES, CHORUS, MESSENGER.

ETEOCLES
Go thou, and bring hither Creon son of Menœceus, the brother of my mother Jocasta, saying this, that I wish to communicate with him counsels of a private nature and those which concern the common welfare of the country, before we go into battle and the ranks of war. And see, he spares the trouble of your steps, by his presence; for I see him coming toward my palace.

CREON, ETEOCLES, CHORUS.

CREON
Surely have I visited many places, desiring to see you, O king Eteocles! and I have gone round to the gates and the guards of the Thebans, seeking you.

ETEOCLES
And indeed I have wished to see you, Creon, for I found attempts at reconciliation altogether fail when I came and entered into conference with Polynices.

CREON
I have heard that he aspires to higher thoughts than Thebes, having trusted in his alliance with Adrastus and his army. But it becomes us to hold these things in dependence on the Gods. But what is most immediately before us, this am I come to acquaint you with.

ETEOCLES

What is this? for I understand not your speech.

CREON

A prisoner is arrived from the Argives.

ETEOCLES

Does he bring us any news of those stationed there?

CREON

The Argive army is preparing quickly to surround the city of the Thebans with thickly-ranged arms.

ETEOCLES

Therefore must we draw our forces out of the Theban city.

CREON

Whither? Dost thou not in the impetuosity of youth see what it behooves thee to see?

ETEOCLES

Without these trenches, as we are quickly about to fight.

CREON

Small are the forces of this land; but theirs innumerable.

ETEOCLES

I know that they are bold in words.

CREON

Argos of the Greeks has some renown.

ETEOCLES

Be confident; quickly will I fill the plain with their slaughter.

CREON

I would it were so: but this I see is a work of much labor.

ETEOCLES

Know that I will not restrain my forces within the walls.

CREON

And yet the whole of victory is prudence.

ETEOCLES

Dost thou wish then that I have recourse to other measures?

CREON

To every measure indeed, rather than hazard all on one battle.

ETEOCLES

What if we were to attack them by night from ambush?

CREON
If, having failed, at least you can have a safe retreat hither.

ETEOCLES
Night brings the same advantage to all, but more to the daring.

CREON
Dreadful is it to fail in the darkness of night.

ETEOCLES
But shall I lead my force against them while at their meal?

CREON
That would cause terror; but we must conquer.

ETEOCLES
The ford of Dirce is indeed deep to pass.

CREON
Every thing is inferior to a good guard.

ETEOCLES
What then, shall I charge the Argive army with my cavalry?

CREON
And there the army is fenced round with chariots.

ETEOCLES
What then shall I do? give up the city to the enemy?

CREON
By no means; but deliberate if thou art wise.

ETEOCLES
What more prudent forethought is there?

CREON
They say that they have seven men, as I have heard.

ETEOCLES
What have they been commanded to do? for their strength is small.

CREON
To head their bands, to besiege the seven gates.

ETEOCLES
What then shall we do? I will not wait this indecision.

CREON
Do thou thyself also choose seven men for the gates.

ETEOCLES

To head divisions, or for single combat?

CREON

To head divisions, having selected the bravest.

ETEOCLES

I understand you; to guard the approach to the walls.

CREON

And with them other generals; one man sees not every thing?

ETEOCLES

Having chosen them for boldness, or prudence in judgment?

CREON

For both; for one without the other availeth nothing.

ETEOCLES

It shall be so: and having gone to the city of the seven towers, I will appoint chiefs at the gates, as you advise, having opposed equal champions against equal foes. But to mention the name of each would be a great delay, the enemy encamped under our very walls. But I will go, that I may not be idle with my hand. And may it befall me to find my brother opposed to me, and being joined with me in battle, to take him with my spear, and to slay him, who came to desolate my country. But it is thy duty to attend to the marriage of my sister Antigone and thy son Hæmon, if I fail aught of success; but the firm vow made before I now confirm at my going out. Thou art my mother's brother, why need I use more words? Treat her worthily, both for thine own and my sake. But my father incurs the punishment of the rashness he brought upon himself, having quenched his sight; I praise him not; even us will he put to death with his execrations, should he gain his point. But one thing is left undone by us, if the soothsayer Tiresias have any oracle to deliver, to enquire this of him; but I will send thy son, Creon, Menœceus, of the same name with thy father, to bring Tiresias hither. With pleasure will he enter into conversation with you; but I lately reviled him with his divining art, so that he is offended with me. But this charge I give the city with thee, Creon; if my arms should conquer, that the body of Polynices be never buried in this Theban land; but that the man who buries him shall die, although he be a friend. This I have told you: but my attendants I tell, bring out my arms, and my panoply which covers me, that we may go this appointed contest of the spear with victorious justice. But to Caution, the most valued of the Goddesses, will we address our prayers to preserve this city.

CHORUS

O Mars, cause of infinite woe, why, I pray, art thou so possessed with blood and death, so discordant with the revels of Bacchus? Thou dost not in the circle of beautiful dancers in the bloom of youth, having let flow thy hair, on the breath of the flute modulate strains, in which there is a lovely power to renew the dance. But with thy armed men, having excited the army of Argives against Thebes with blood, thou dancest before the city in a most inharmonious revel, thou movest not thy foot maddened by the thyrsus clad in fawn-skins, but thy solid-hoofed steed with thy chariot and horses' bits; and bounding at the streams of Ismenus, thou art borne rapidly in the chariot-course, having excited against the race of those sown by Cadmus, a raging host that grasp the shield, well armed, adverse to us at the walls of stone: surely Discord is some dreadful Goddess, who devised all these calamities against the princes of this land, the Labdacidæ involved in woe. O thou forest of heavenly foliage, most productive of beasts, thou snowy eye of Diana, Cithæron, never oughtest thou to have nourished him doomed to death, the son of Jocasta, Œdipus, the babe who was cast out from his home, marked by the golden clasps. Neither ought that winged virgin the Sphinx, thou mountain monster, that grief to this land, to have come, with her most inharmonious lays; who formerly approaching our walls, bore in her four talons the descendants of Cadmus to the inaccessible light of heaven, whom the infernal Pluto sends against the Thebans; but other ill-fated discord among the children of Œdipus springs up in the palace and in the city. For that which is not honorable, never can be honorable, as neither can children the unhallowed offspring of the mother, the pollution of the father. But she came to a kindred bed. Thou didst produce, O Theban land! thou didst produce formerly (as I heard the foreign report, I heard it formerly at home), the race sprung from teeth from the fiery-crested dragon fed on beasts, the proudest honor of Thebes. But to the nuptials of Harmonia the Gods came of old, and by the harp and by the lyre of Amphion uprose the walls of Thebes the tower of the double streams, at the midst of the pass of Dirce, which waters the verdant plain before Ismenus. And Io, our ancient mother, doomed to bear horns, brought forth a line of Theban kings. But this city receiving ten thousand goods one in change for another, hath stood in the highest chaplets of war.

TIRESIAS (Led by his **DAUGHTER**), **MENŒCEUS, CREON, CHORUS**.

TIRESIAS
Lead onward, my daughter, since thou art an eye to my blind steps, as the star to the mariners. Placing my steps hither on this level plain, proceed lest we stumble; thy father is feeble; and preserve carefully in thy virgin hand my calculations which I took, having learned the auguries of the birds, sitting in the sacred seats where I fortell the future. My child, Menœceus, son of Creon, tell me, how far is the remainder of the journey through the city to thy father? Since my knees are weary, and with difficulty I accomplish such a long journey.

CREON
Be of good cheer; for thou hast steered thy foot, Tiresias, near to thy friends; but take hold of him, my son. Since every chariot, and the foot of the aged man is used to expect the assistance of another's hand.

TIRESIAS
Well: I am present; but why didst thou call me with such haste, Creon?

CREON
We have not as yet forgotten: but recover thy strength, and collect thy breath, having thrown aside the fatigue occasioned by the journey.

TIRESIAS
I am relaxed indeed with toil, brought hither from the Athenians the day before this. For there also was a contest of the spear with Eumolpus, where I made the descendants of Cecrops splendid conquerors. And I wear this golden chaplet, as thou seest, having received the first-fruits of the spoil of the enemy.

CREON
Thy victorious garlands I make a happy omen. For we, as thou well knowest, are tossing in a storm of war with the Greeks, and great is the hazard of Thebes. The king Eteocles has therefore gone forth adorned with his armor already to battle with the Argives. But to me has he sent that I might learn from you, by doing what we should be most likely to preserve the city.

TIRESIAS

For Eteocles' sake indeed I would have stopped my mouth, and repressed the oracles, but to thee, since thou desirest to know them, will I declare them: for this land labors under the malady of old, O Creon, from the time when Laïus became the father of children in spite of the Gods, and begat the wretched Œdipus, a husband for his mother. But the cruel lacerations of his eyes were in the wisdom of the Gods, and a warning to Greece. Which things the sons of Œdipus seeking to conceal among themselves by the lapse of time, as about forsooth to escape from the Gods, erred through their ignorance, for they neither giving the honor due to their father, nor allowing him a free liberty, infuriated the unfortunate man: and he breathed out against them dreadful threats, being both in affliction, and moreover dishonored. And I, what things omitting to do, and what words omitting to speak on the subject, have nevertheless fallen into the hatred of the sons of Œdipus? But death from their mutual hands is near them, O Creon. And many corses fallen around corses, having mingled the weapons of Argos and Thebes, shall cause bitter lamentations to the Theban land. And thou, O wretched city, art sapped from thy foundations, unless men will obey my words. For this were the first thing, that not any of the family of Œdipus should be citizens, nor king of the territory, inasmuch as they are possessed by demons, and are they that will overthrow the city. And since the evil triumphs over the good, there is one other thing requisite to insure preservation. But, as this is neither safe for me to say, and distressing to those on whom the lot has fallen, to give to the city the balm of preservation, I will depart: farewell; for being an individual with many shall I suffer what is about to happen if it must be so; for what can I do!

CREON

Stay here, old man.

TIRESIAS

Lay not hold upon me.

CREON

Remain; why dost thou fly me?

TIRESIAS

Thy fortune flies thee, but not I.

CREON

Tell me the means of preserving the citizens and their city.

TIRESIAS

Thou wishest now indeed, and soon thou wilt not wish.

CREON

And how am I not willing to preserve my country?

TIRESIAS

Art thou willing then to hear, and art thou eager?

CREON

For toward what ought I to have a greater eagerness?

TIRESIAS

Hear now then my prophecies.—But this first I wish to ascertain clearly, where is Menœceus who brought me hither.

CREON

He is not far off, but close to thee.

TIRESIAS

Let him depart then afar from my oracles.

CREON

He that is my son will keep secret what ought to be kept secret.

TIRESIAS

Art thou willing then that I speak in his presence?

CREON

Yes: for he would be delighted to hear of the means of preservation.

TIRESIAS

Hear now then the tenor of my oracles; what things doing ye may preserve the city of the Cadmeans. It is necessary for thee to sacrifice this thy son Menœceus for the country, since thou thyself callest for this fortune.

CREON

What sayest thou, what word is this thou hast spoken, old man?

TIRESIAS

As circumstances are, thus also oughtest thou to act.

CREON

O thou, that hast said many evils in a short time!

TIRESIAS

To thee at least; but to thy country great and salutary.

CREON

I heard not, I attended not; let the city go where it will.

TIRESIAS

This is no longer the same man; he retracts again what he said.

CREON

Farewell! depart; for I have no need of thy prophecies.

TIRESIAS

Has truth perished, because thou art unfortunate?

CREON

By thy knees I implore thee, and by thy reverend locks.

TIRESIAS

Why kneel to me? the evils thou askest are hard to be controlled.

CREON

Keep it secret; and speak not these words to the city.

TIRESIAS

Dost thou command me to be unjust? I can not be silent.

CREON

What then wilt thou do to me? Wilt thou slay my son?

TIRESIAS

These things will be a care to others; but by me will it be spoken.

CREON

But from whence has this evil come to me, and to my child?

TIRESIAS

Well dost thou ask me, and comest to the drift of my discourse. It is necessary that he, stabbed in that cave where the earth-born dragon lay, the guardian of Dirce's fountain, give his gory blood a libation to the earth on account of the ancient wrath of Mars against Cadmus, who avenges the slaughter of the earth-born dragon; and these things done, ye shall obtain Mars as your ally. But if the earth receive fruit in return for fruit, and mortal blood in return for blood, ye shall have that land propitious, which formerly sent forth a crop of men from seed armed with golden helmets; but there must of this race die one, who is the son of the dragon's jaw. But thou art left among us of the race of those sown men, pure in thy descent, both by thy mother's side and in the male line; and thy children too: Hæmon's marriage however precludes his being slain, for he is not a youth, for, although he has not approached her bed, he has yet contracted the marriage. But this youth, devoted to this city, by dying may preserve his native country. And he will cause a bitter return to Adrastus and the Argives, casting back death over their eyes, and Thebes will he make illustrious: of these two fates choose the one; either preserve thy child or the state. Every information from me thou hast:—lead me, my child, toward home;—but whoever exercises the art of divination, is a fool; if indeed he chance to show disagreeable things, he is rendered hateful to those to whom he may prophesy; but speaking falsely to his employers from motives of pity, he is unjust as touching the Gods.—Phœbus alone should speak in oracles to men, who fears nobody.

CREON, MENŒCEUS, CHORUS.

CHORUS

Creon, why art thou mute compressing thy voice in silence, for to me also there is no less consternation.

CREON

But what can one say?—It is clear however what my answer will be. For never will I go to this degree of calamity, to expose my son a victim for the state. For all men live with an affection toward their children, nor would any give up his own child to die. Let no one praise me for the deed, and slay my children. But I myself, for I am arrived at a mature period of life, am ready to die to liberate my country. But haste, my son, before the whole city hears it, disregarding the intemperate oracles of prophets, fly as quickly as possible, having quitted this land. For he will tell these things to the authorities and chiefs, going to the seven gates, and to the officers: and if indeed we get before him, there is safety for thee, but if thou art too late, we are undone, thou diest.

MENŒCEUS

Whither then fly? To what city? what friends?

CREON
Wheresoever thou wilt be farthest removed from this country.

MENŒCEUS
Therefore it is fitting for thee to speak, and for me to do.

CREON
Having passed through Delphi—

MENŒCEUS
Whither is it right for me to go, my father?

CREON
To the land of Ætolia.

MENŒCEUS
And from this whither shall I proceed?

CREON
To Thesprotia's soil.

MENŒCEUS
To the sacred seat of Dodona?

CREON
Thou understandest.

MENŒCEUS
What then will there be to protect me?

CREON
The conducting deity.

MENŒCEUS
But what means of procuring money?

CREON
I will supply gold.

MENŒCEUS
Thou sayest well, my father. Go then, for having proceeded to salute34 thy sister, whose breast I first sucked, Jocasta I mean, deprived of my mother, and reft from her, an orphan, I will depart and save my life. But haste, go, let not thy purpose be hindered.

MENŒCEUS, CHORUS.

MENŒCEUS
Ye females, how well removed I my father's fears, having deceived him with words, in order to gain my wishes; who sends me out of the way, depriving the city of its good fortune, and gives me up to

cowardice. And these things are pardonable indeed in an old man, but in my case it deserves no pardon to become the deserter of that country which gave me birth. That ye may know then, I will go, and preserve the city, and will give up my life for this land. For it is a disgraceful thing, that those indeed who are free from the oracle, and are not concerned with any compulsion of the Gods, standing at their shields in battle, shall not be slow to die fighting before the towers for their country; and I, having betrayed my father, and my brother, and my own city, shall depart coward-like from out of the land; but wherever I live, I shall appear vile. No: by that Jove that dwelleth amidst the constellations, and sanguinary Mars, who set up those sown men, who erst sprung from the earth, to be kings of this country. But I will depart, and standing on the summit of the battlements, stabbing myself over the dark deep lair of the dragon, where the prophet appointed, will give liberty to the country—the word has been spoken. But I go, by my death about to give no mean gift to the state, and will rid this land of its affliction. For if every one, seizing what opportunity he had in his power of doing good, would persist in it, and bring it forward for his country's weal, states, experiencing fewer calamities, henceforward might be prosperous.

CHORUS
Thou camest forth, thou camest forth, O winged monster, production of the earth, and the viper of hell, the ravager of the Cadmeans, big with destruction, big with woes, in form half-virgin, a hostile prodigy, with thy ravening wings, and thy talons that preyed on raw flesh, who erst from Dirce's spot bearing aloft the youths, accompanied by an inharmonious lay, thou broughtest, thou broughtest cruel woes to our country; cruel was he of the Gods, whoever was the author of these things. And the moans of the matrons, and the moans of the virgins, resounded in the house, in a voice, in a strain of misery, they lamented some one thing, some another, in succession through the city. And the groaning and the noise was like to thunder, when the winged virgin bore out of sight any man from the city. But at length came by the mission of the Pythian oracle Œdipus the unhappy to this land of Thebes, to us then indeed delighted, but again came woes. For he, wretched man, having gained the glorious victory over the enigmas, contracts a marriage, an unfortunate marriage with his mother, and pollutes the city. And fresh woes does the unfortunate man cause to succeed with slaughter, devoting by curses his sons to the unhallowed contest.—With admiration, with admiration we look on him, who is gone to kill himself for the sake of his country's land; to Creon indeed having left lamentations, but about to make the seven-towered gates of the land greatly victorious. Thus may we be mothers, thus may we be blest in our children, O dear Pallas, who destroyedst the blood of the dragon by the hurled stone, driving the attention of Cadmus to the action, whence with rapine some fiend of the Gods rushed on this land.

MESSENGER, JOCASTA, CHORUS.

MESSENGER
Ho there! who is at the gate of the palace? Open, conduct Jocasta from out of the house.—What ho! again—after a long time indeed, but yet come forth, hear, O renowned wife of Œdipus, ceasing from thy lamentations, and thy tears of grief.

JOCASTA
O most dear man, surely thou comest bearing the news of some calamity, of the death of Eteocles, by whose shield thou always didst go, warding off the weapons of the enemy. What new message, I pray, dost thou come to deliver? Is my son dead or alive? Tell me.

MESSENGER
He lives, be not alarmed for this, for I will rid thee of this fear.

JOCASTA

But what? In what state are our seven-towered ramparts?

MESSENGER
They stand unshaken, nor is the city destroyed.

JOCASTA
Come they in danger from the spear of Argos?

MESSENGER
To the very extreme of danger; but the arms of Thebes came off superior to the Mycenæan spear.

JOCASTA
Tell me one thing, by the Gods, whether thou knowest any thing of Polynices (since this is a concern to me also) whether he sees the light.

MESSENGER
Thus far in the day thy pair of children lives.

JOCASTA
Be thou blest. But how did ye stationed on the towers drive off the spear of Argos from the gates? Tell me, that I may go and delight the old blind man in the house with the news of his country's being preserved.

MESSENGER
After that the son of Creon, he that died for the land, standing on the summit of the towers, plunged the black-handled sword into his throat, the salvation of this land, thy son placed seven cohorts, and their leaders with them, at the seven gates, guards against the Argive spear; and he drew up the horse ready to support the horse, and the heavy-armed men to reinforce the shield-bearers, so that to the part of the wall which was in danger there might be succor at hand. But from the lofty citadel we view the army of the Argives with their white shields, having quitted Tumessus and now come near the trench, at full speed they reached the city of the land of Cadmus. And the pæan and the trumpets at the same time from them resounded, and off the walls from us. And first indeed Parthenopæus the son of the huntress (Atalanta) led his division horrent with their thick shields against the Neïtan gate, having a family device in the middle of his shield, Atalanta destroying the Ætolian boar with her distant-wounding bow. And against the Prætan gate marched the prophet Amphiaraüs, having victims in his car, not bearing an insolent emblem, but modestly having his arms without a device. But against the Ogygian gate stood Prince Hippomedon, bearing an emblem in the middle of his shield, the Argus gazing with his spangled eyes, some eyes indeed with the rising of the stars awake, and some with the setting closed, as we had the opportunity of seeing afterward when he was dead. But Tydeus was drawn up at the Homoloïan gate, having on his shield a lion's skin rough with his mane, but in his right hand he bore a torch, as the Titan Prometheus, intent on firing the city. But thy son Polynices drew up his array at the Crenean gate; but the swift Potnian mares, the emblem on his shield, were starting through fright, well circularly grouped within the orb at the handle of the shield, so that they seemed infuriated. But Capaneus, not holding less notions than Mars on the approaching battle, drew up his division against the Electran gate. Upon the iron embossments of his shield was an earth-born giant bearing upon his shoulders a whole city, which he had torn up from the foundations with bars, an intimation to us what our city should suffer. But at the seventh gate was Adrastus, having his shield filled with a hundred vipers, bearing on his left arm a representation of the hydra, the boast of Argos, and from the midst of the walls the dragons were bearing the children of the Thebans in their jaws. But I had the opportunity of seeing each of these, as I took the word of battle to the leaders of the divisions. And first indeed we fought with

bows, and javelins, and distant-wounding slings, and fragments of rocks; but when we were conquering in the fight, Tydeus shouted out, and thy son on a sudden, "O sons of the Danaï, why delay we, ere we are galled with their missile weapons, to make a rush at the gates all in a body, light-armed men, horsemen, and those who drive the chariots?" And when they heard the cry, no one was backward; but many fell, their heads besmeared with blood; of us also you might have seen before the walls frequent divers toppling to the ground; and they moistened the parched earth with streams of blood. But the Arcadian, no Argive, the son of Atalanta, as some whirlwind falling on the gates, calls out for fire and a spade, as though he would dig up the city. But Periclymenus the son of the God of the Ocean stopped him in his raging, hurling at his head a stone, a wagon-load, a pinnacle rent from the battlement; and dashed in pieces his head with its auburn hair, and crushed the suture of the bones, and besmeared with blood his lately blooming cheeks; nor shall he carry back his living form to his mother, glorious in her bow, the daughter of Mænalus. But when thy son saw this gate was in a state of safety, he went to another, and I followed. But I see Tydeus, and many armed with shields around him, darting with their Ætolian lances at the highest battlements of the towers, so that our men put to flight quitted the heights of the ramparts; but thy son, as a hunter, collects them together again; and posted them a second time on the towers; and we hasten on to another gate, having relieved the distress in this quarter. But Capaneus, how can I express the measure of his rage! For he came bearing the ranges of a long-reaching ladder, and made this high boast, "That not even the hallowed fire of Jove should hinder him from taking the city from its highest turrets." And these things soon as he had proclaimed, though assailed with stones, he clambered up, having contracted his body under his shield, climbing the slippery footing of the bars of the ladder: but when he was now mounting the battlements of the walls Jupiter strikes him with his thunder; and the earth resounded, insomuch that all trembled; and his limbs were hurled, as it were by a sling, from the ladder separately from one another, his hair to heaven, and his blood to the ground, and his limbs, like the whirling of Ixion on his wheel, were carried round; and his scorched body falls to the earth. But when Adrastus saw that Jove was hostile to his army, he stationed the host of the Argives without the trench. But ours on the contrary, when they saw the auspicious sign from Jove, drove out their chariots, horsemen and heavy-armed, and rushing into the midst of the Argive arms engaged in fight: and there were all the sorts of misery together: they died, they fell from their chariots, and the wheels leaped up and axles upon axles: and corses were heaped together with corses.—We have preserved then our towers from being overthrown to this present day; but whether for the future this land will be prosperous, rests with the Gods.

CHORUS
To conquer is glorious; but if the Gods have the better intent, may I be fortunate!

JOCASTA
Well are the ways of the Gods, and of fortune; for my children live, and my country has escaped; but the unhappy Creon seems to feel the effects of my marriage, and of Œdipus's misfortunes, being deprived of his child; for the state indeed, happily, but individually, to his misery: but recount to me again, what after this did my two sons purpose to do?

MESSENGER
Forbear the rest; for in every circumstance hitherto thou art fortunate.

JOCASTA
This hast thou said so as to raise suspicion; I must not forbear.

MESSENGER
Dost thou want any thing more than that thy sons are safe?

JOCASTA

In what follows also I would hear if I am fortunate.

MESSENGER

Let me go: thy son is deprived of his armor-bearer.

JOCASTA

Thou concealest some ill and coverest it in obscurity.

MESSENGER

I can not speak thy ills after thy happiness.

JOCASTA

But thou shalt, unless fleeing from me thou fleest through the air.

MESSENGER

Alas! alas! Why dost thou not suffer me to depart after a message of glad tidings, but forcest me to tell calamities?—Thy sons are intent on most shameful deeds of boldness—to engage in single combat apart from the whole army, having addressed to the Argives and Thebans in common a speech, such as they never ought to have spoken. But Eteocles began, standing on the lofty turret, having commanded to proclaim silence to the army. And he said, "O generals of the Grecian land, and chieftains of the Danaï, who have come hither, and O people of Cadmus, neither for the sake of Polynices barter your lives, nor for my cause. For I myself, taking this danger on myself, alone will enter the lists with my brother; and if indeed I slay him, I will dwell in the palace alone; but should I be subdued, I will give it up to him alone. But you, ceasing from the combat, O Argives, shall return to your land, not leaving your lives here; of the Theban people also there is enough that lieth dead," Thus much he spake; but thy son Polynices rushed from the ranks, and approved his words. But all the Argives murmured their applause, and the people of Cadmus, as thinking this plan just. And after this the generals made a truce, and in the space between the two armies pledged an oath to abide by it. And now the two sons of the aged Œdipus clad their bodies in an entire suit of brazen armor. And their friends adorned them, the champion of this land indeed the chieftains of the Thebans; and him the principal men of the Danaï. And they stood resplendent, and they changed not their color, raging to let forth their spears at each other. But their friends on either side as they passed by encouraging them with words, thus spoke. "Polynices, it rests with thee to erect the statue of Jove, emblem of victory, and to confer a glorious fame on Argos." But to Eteocles on the other hand; "Now thou fightest for the state, now if thou come off victorious, thou art in possession of the sceptre." These things they said exhorting them to the combat. But the seers sacrificed the sheep, and scrutinized the shooting of the flames, and the bursting of the gall, the moisture adverse to the fire, and the extremity of the flame, which bears a two-fold import, both the sign of victory, and the sign of being defeated. But if thou hast any power, or words of wisdom, or the soothing charms of incantation, go, stay thy children from the fearful combat, since great the danger, and dreadful will be the sequel of the contest, namely, tears for thee, deprived this day of thy two children.

JOCASTA

O my child, Antigone, come forth from before the palace; the state of thy fortune suits not now the dance, nor the virgin's chamber, but it is thy duty, in conjunction with thy mother, to hinder two excellent men, and thy brothers verging toward death from falling by each other's hands.

ANTIGONE, JOCASTA, CHORUS.

ANTIGONE

With what new horrors, O mother of my being, dost thou call out to thy friends before the house?

JOCASTA
O my daughter, the life of thy brothers is gone from them.

ANTIGONE
How sayest thou?

JOCASTA
They are drawn out in single combat.

ANTIGONE
Alas me! what wilt thou say, my mother?

JOCASTA
Nothing of pleasant import; but follow.

ANTIGONE
Whither? leaving my virgin chamber.

JOCASTA
To the army.

ANTIGONE
I am ashamed to go among the crowd.

JOCASTA
Thy present state admits not bashfulness.

ANTIGONE
But what shall I do then?

JOCASTA
Thou shalt quell the strife of the brothers.

ANTIGONE
Doing what, my mother.

JOCASTA
Falling before them with me.

ANTIGONE
Lead to the space between the armies; we must not delay.

JOCASTA
Haste, daughter, haste, since, if indeed I reach my sons before they engage, I still exist in heaven's fair light, but if they die, I shall lie dead with them.

CHORUS
Alas! alas! shuddering with horror, shuddering is my breast; and through my flesh came pity, pity for the unhappy mother, on account of her two children, whether of them then will distain with blood

the other (alas me for my sufferings, O Jove, O earth), the own brother's neck, the own brother's life, in arms, in slaughter? Wretched, wretched I, over which corse then shall I raise the lamentation for the dead? O earth, earth, the two beasts of prey, blood-thirsty souls, brandishing the spear, will quickly distain with blood the fallen, fallen enemy. Wretches, that they ever came to the thought of a single combat! In a foreign strain will I mourn with tears my elegy of groans due to the dead. Destiny is at hand—death is near; this day will decide the event. Ill-fated, ill-fated murder because of the Furies! But I see Creon here with clouded brow advancing toward the house, I will cease therefore from the groans I am uttering.

CREON, CHORUS.

CREON
Ah me! what shall I do? whether am I to groan in weeping myself, or the city, which a cloud of such magnitude encircles as to cast us amidst the gloom of Acheron? For my son has perished having died for the city, having achieved a glorious name, but to me a name of sorrow. Him having taken just now from the dragon's den, stabbed by his own hand, I wretched bore in my arms; and the whole house resounds with shrieks; but I, myself aged, am come after my aged sister Jocasta, that she may wash and lay out my son now no more. For it behooves the living well to revere the God below by paying honors to the dead.

CHORUS
Thy sister is gone out of the house, O Creon, and the girl Antigone attending the steps of her mother.

CREON
Whither? and for what hap? tell me.

CHORUS
She heard that her sons were about to come to a contest in single battle for the royal palace.

CREON
How sayest thou? whilst I was fondly attending to my son's corse, I arrived not so far in knowledge, as to be acquainted with this also.

CHORUS
But thy sister has indeed been gone some time; but I think, O Creon, that the contest, in which their lives are at stake, has already been concluded by the sons of Œdipus.

CREON
Ah me! I see indeed this signal, the downcast eye and countenance of the approaching messenger, who will relate every thing that has taken place.

MESSENGER, CREON, CHORUS.

MESSENGER
O wretched me! what language or what words can I utter? We are undone—

CREON
Thou beginnest thy speech with no promising prelude.

MESSENGER
Oh wretched me! doubly do I lament, for I hear great calamities.

CREON

In addition to the calamities that have happened dost thou still speak of others?

MESSENGER

Thy sister's sons, O Creon, no longer behold the light.

CREON

Ah! alas! thou utterest great ills to me and to the state.

MESSENGER

O mansions of Œdipus, do ye hear these things of thy children who have perished by similar fates?

CHORUS

Ay, so that, had they but sense, they would weep.

CREON

O most heavy misery! Oh me wretched with woes! alas! unhappy me!

MESSENGER

If that thou knewest the evils yet in addition to these.

CREON

And how can there be more fatal ills than these?

MESSENGER

Thy sister is dead with her two children.

CHORUS

Raise, raise the cry of woe, and smite your heads with the blows of your white hands.

CREON

Oh unhappy Jocasta, what an end of thy life and of thy marriage hast thou endured in the riddles of the Sphinx! But how took place the slaughter of her two sons, and the combat arising from the curse of Œdipus? Tell me.

MESSENGER

The success of the country before the towers indeed thou knowest; for the circuit of the wall is not of such vast extent, but that thou must know all that has taken place. But after that the sons of the aged Œdipus had clad their limbs in brazen armor, they came and stood in the midst of the plain between the two armies, ready for the contest, and the fierceness of the single battle. And having cast a look toward Argos, Polynices uttered his prayer; "O venerable Juno (for I am thine, since in marriage I joined myself with the daughter of Adrastus, and dwell in that land), grant me to slay my brother, and to cover with blood my hostile hand bearing the victory." And Eteocles looking at the temple of Pallas, glorious in her golden shield, prayed; "O Daughter of Jove, grant me with my hand to hurl my victorious spear from this arm home to the breast of my brother, and slay him who came to lay waste my country." And when the sound of the Tuscan trumpet was raised, as the torch, the signal for the fierce battle, they sped with dreadful rush toward each other; and like wild boars whetting their savage tusks, they met, their cheeks all moist with foam; and they rushed forward with their lances; but they couched beneath the orbs of their shields, in order that the steel might fall harmless. But if either perceived the other's eye raised above the verge, he drove the lance at his face, intent to be beforehand with him: but dexterously they shifted their eyes to the open ornaments of their shields, so that the spear was made of none effect. And more sweat trickled down the spectators than the combatants, through the fear of their friends. But Eteocles, stumbling with his foot against a stone, which rolled under his tread, places his limb without the shield. But Polynices ran up with his spear, when he saw a stroke open to his steel, and the Argive spear passed through the shank. And all the host of the Danaï shouted for joy. And the hero who first was wounded, when he perceived his shoulder exposed in this effort, pierced the breast of Polynices with his lance, and gave joy to the citizens of Cadmus, but he broke the point of his spear. But being come to a strait for a spear, he retreated backward on his leg, and taking a stone of marble, he hurled it and crashed his antagonist's spear in the middle: and the battle was on equal terms, both being deprived of the spear in their hands. Then seizing the handles of their swords they met at close quarters, and, as they clashed their shields together, raised a great tumult of battle around them. And Eteocles having a sort of idea of its success, made use of a Thessalian stratagem, which he had learned from his connection with that country. For giving up his present mode of attack, he brings his left foot behind, protecting well the pit of his own stomach; and stepping forward his right leg, he plunged the sword through the navel, and drove it to the vertebræ. But the unhappy Polynices bending together his side and his bowels falls weltering in blood. But the other, as he were now the victor, and had subdued him in the fight, casting his sword on the ground, went to spoil him, not fixing his attention on himself, but on that his purpose. Which thing also deceived him; for Polynices, he that fell first, still breathing a little, preserving his sword e'en in his deathly fall, with difficulty indeed, but he did stretch his sword to the heart of Eteocles. And holding the dust in their gripe they both fall near one another, and determined not the victory.

CHORUS
Alas! alas! to what degree, O Œdipus, do I groan for thy misfortunes! but the God seems to have fulfilled thy imprecations.

MESSENGER
Hear now then woes even in addition to these—For when her sons having fallen were breathing their last, at this moment the wretched mother rushes before them, and when she perceived them stricken with mortal wounds she shrieked out, "Oh my sons, I am come too late a succor:" and throwing herself by the side of her children in turn, she wept, she lamented with moans her long anxiety in suckling them now lost: and their sister, who accompanied to stand by her in her misery, at the same time broke forth; "O supporters of my mother's age! Oh ye that have betrayed my hopes of marriage, my dearest brothers!"—But king Eteocles heaving from his breast his gasping breath, heard his mother, and putting out his cold clammy hand, sent not forth indeed a voice; but from his eyes spoke her in tears to signify affection. But Polynices, who yet breathed, looking at his sister and his aged mother, thus spoke: "We perish, O my mother; but I grieve for thee, and for this my sister, and my brother who lies dead, for being my friend, he became my enemy, but still my friend.—But bury me, O mother of my being, and thou my sister, in my native land, and pacify the exasperated city, that I may obtain thus much at least of my country's land, although I have lost the palace. And close my eyelids with thy hand, my mother" (and he places it himself upon his eyes), "and fare ye well! for now darkness surroundeth me." And both breathed out their lives together. And the mother, when she saw what had taken place, beyond endurance grieving, snatched the sword from the dead body, and perpetrated a deed of horror; for she drove the steel through the middle of her throat, and lies dead on those most dear to her, having each in her arms embraced. But the people rose up hastily to a strife of opinions; we indeed, as holding, that my master was victorious; but they, that the other was; and there was also a contention between the generals, those on the other side contended, that Polynices first struck with the spear, but those on ours that there was no victory where the combatants died. And in the mean time Antigone withdrew from the army; but they rushed to arms; but fortunately by a sort of foresight the people of Cadmus had sat

upon their shields: and we gained the advantage of falling on the Argives not yet accoutred in their arms. And no one made a stand, but flying they covered the plain; and immense quantities of blood were spilt of the corses that fell, but when we were victorious in the fight, some indeed raised the image of Jove emblem of victory, but some of us stripping the shields from the Argive corses sent the spoils within the city. But others with Antigone are bearing hither the dead for their friends to lament over. But these contests have in some respect turned out most happy for this state, but in other respect most unhappy.

CHORUS
No longer the misfortunes of the house come to our ears, we may also see before the palace these three fallen corses, who have shared the dark realms by a united death.

[The dead bodies borne.

ANTIGONE, CREON, CHORUS.

ANTIGONE
Not veiling the softness of my cheek on which my ringlets fall, nor caring for the purple glow of virginity under my lids, the blush of my countenance, I am borne along the bacchanal of the dead, rending the fillet from my hair, rejecting the saffron robe of delicateness, having the mournful office of conducting the dead. Alas! alas! woe is me! Oh Polynices, thou well answeredst to thy name! Alas me! Oh Thebes! but thy strife, no strife, but murder consummated with murder, hath destroyed the house of Œdipus with dreadful, with mournful blood. But what groan responsive to my sufferings, or what lament of music shall I invoke to my tears, to my tears, O house, O house, bearing these three kindred bodies, my mother, and her children, the joy of the fury? who destroyed the entire house of Œdipus, what time intelligently he unfolded the difficult song of the fierce monster, having thereby slain the body of the fierce musical Sphinx. Alas me! my father; what Grecian, or what Barbarian, or what other of the noble in birth, of mortal blood, in time of old ever bore such manifest sufferings of so many ills? Wretched I, how do I lament! What bird, sitting on the highest boughs of the oak or pine, will sing responsive to my lamentations, who have lost my mother? who weep the strain of grief in addition to these moans for my brothers, about to pass my long life in floods of tears.— Which shall I bewail? On which first shall I scatter the first offerings rent from my hair? On my mother's two breasts of milk, or upon the death-wounds of my two brothers? Alas! alas! Leave thine house, bringing thy sightless eye, O aged father, Œdipus, show thy wretched age, who within thy palace having poured the gloomy darkness over thine eyes, draggest on a long life. Dost thou hear wandering in the hall,—resting thy aged foot upon the couch in a state of misery?

ŒDIPUS, CREON, ANTIGONE, CHORUS.

ŒDIPUS
Why, O virgin, hast thou with the most doleful tears called me forth leaning on the support of a blind foot to the light, a bed-ridden man from his darksome chamber, gray-headed, an obscure phantom of air—a dead body beneath the earth—a flitting dream?

ANTIGONE
O father, thou shalt receive words of unhappy tidings; no longer do thy children behold the light, nor thy wife, who ever was employed in attending as a staff on thy blind foot, my father: alas me!

ŒDIPUS
Alas me, for my sufferings! for well may I groan and vociferate these things. The three souls, tell me, my child, by what fate, how quitted they this light?

ANTIGONE

Not for the sake of reproaching thee, nor exulting over thee, but for grief I speak: thy evil genius, heavy with swords, and fire, and wretched combats, has rushed down upon thy children, O my father.

ŒDIPUS

Alas me! ah! ah!

ANTIGONE

Why dost thou thus groan?

ŒDIPUS

Alas me! my children!

ANTIGONE

Thou wouldest grieve indeed, if looking on the chariot of the sun drawn by its four steeds, thou couldest direct the sight of thine eyes to these bodies of the dead.

ŒDIPUS

The evil of my sons indeed is manifest; but my wretched wife, by what fate, O my child, did she perish?

ANTIGONE

Causing to all tears of grief they could not contain, to her children she bared her breast, a suppliant she bared it, holding it up in supplication. But the mother found her children at the Electran gate, in the mead where the lotus abounds, contending with their lances in the common war, as lions bred in the same cave, with the blood-wounds now a cold, a gory libation, which Plato received, and Mars gave. And having seized the brazen-wrought sword from the dead she plunged it into her flesh, but with grief for her children she fell amidst her children. But all these sufferings, O my father, has the God heaped this day upon our house, whoever he be, that adds this consummation.

CHORUS

This day hath been the beginning of many woes to the house of Œdipus; but may life be more fortunate!

CREON

Now indeed cease from your grief, for it is time to think of the sepulture. But hear these words, O Œdipus; Eteocles, thy son, hath given to me the dominion of this land, giving them as a marriage portion to Hæmon, and with them the bed of thy daughter Antigone. I therefore will not suffer thee any longer to dwell in this land. For clearly did Tiresias say, that never, whilst thou dost inhabit this land, will the state be prosperous. But depart; and this I say not from insolence, nor being thine enemy, but on account of thy evil genius, fearing lest the country suffer any harm.

ŒDIPUS

O Fate, from the beginning how wretched and unhappy didst thou form me, if ever other man was formed! whom, even before I came into the light from my mother's womb, when yet unborn Apollo foretold that I should be the murderer of my father Laïus, alas! wretch that I am! And when I was born, again my father who gave me life, seeks to take my life, considering that I was born his enemy: for it was fated that he should die by my hands, and he sends me, poor wretch, as I craved the breast, a prey for the wild beasts: where I was preserved—for would that Cithæron, it ought, had sunk to the bottomless chasms of Tartarus, for that it did not destroy me; but the God fixed it my lot to serve under Polybus my master: but I unhappy man, having slain my own father, ascended the bed of my wretched mother, and begat children, my brothers, whom I destroyed, having received down the curse from Laïus, and given it to my sons. For I was not by nature so utterly devoid of understanding, as to have devised such things against my eyes, and against the life of my children, without the interference of some of the Gods. Well!—what then shall I ill-fated do? who will accompany me the guide of my dark steps? She that lies here dead! living, well know I, she would. But my noble pair of sons? I have no sons.—But still in my vigor can I myself procure my sustenance? Whence?—Why, O Creon, dost thou thus utterly kill me? for kill me thou wilt, if thou shalt cast me out of the land. Yet will I not appear base, stretching my hands around thy knees, for I can not belie my former nobleness, not even though my plight is miserable.

CREON

Well has it been spoken by thee, that thou wilt not touch my knees, but I can not permit thee to dwell in the land. But of these corses, the one we must even now bear to the house; but the body of Polynices cast out unburied beyond the borders of this land. And these things shall be proclaimed to all the Thebans: "whoever shall be found either crowning the corse, or covering it with earth, shall receive death for his offense." But thou, ceasing from the groans for the three dead, retire, Antigone, within the house, and behave as beseems a virgin, expecting the approaching day in which the bed of Hæmon awaits thee.

ANTIGONE

Oh father, in what a state of woes do we miserable beings lie! How do I lament for thee! more than for the dead! For it is not that one of thy ills is heavy, and the other not heavy, but thou art in all things unhappy, my father.—But thee I ask, our new lord, wherefore dost thou insult my father here, banishing him from his country? Why make thy laws against an unhappy corse?

CREON

The determination of Eteocles this, not mine.

ANTIGONE

It is absurd, and thou a fool to enforce it.

CREON

How so? Is it not just to execute injunctions?

ANTIGONE

No, if they are base, at least, and spoken with ill intent.

CREON

What! will he not with justice be given to the dogs?

ANTIGONE

No, for thus do ye not demand of him lawful justice.

CREON

We do; since he was the enemy of the state, who least ought to be an enemy.

ANTIGONE

Hath he not paid then his life to fortune?

CREON

And in his burial too let him now satisfy vengeance.

ANTIGONE

What outrage having committed, if he came after his share of the kingdom?

CREON

This man, that you may know once for all, shall be unburied.

ANTIGONE

I will bury him; even though the city forbid it.

CREON

Thyself then wilt thou at the same time bury near the corse.

ANTIGONE

But that is a glorious thing, for two friends to lie near.

CREON

Lay hold of her, and bear her to the house.

ANTIGONE

By no means—for I will not let go this body.

CREON

The God has decreed it, O virgin, not as thou wilt.

ANTIGONE

And this too is decreed—that the dead be not insulted.

CREON

Around him none shall place the moist dust.

ANTIGONE

Nay, by his mother here Jocasta, I entreat thee, Creon.

CREON

Thou laborest in vain, for thou canst not obtain this.

ANTIGONE

But suffer thou me at any rate to bathe the body.

CREON

This would be one of the things forbidden by the state.

ANTIGONE

But let me put bandages round his cruel wounds.

CREON

In no way shalt thou show respect to this corse.

ANTIGONE

Oh most dear, but I will at least kiss thy lips.

CREON

Thou shalt not prepare calamity against thy wedding by thy lamentations.

ANTIGONE

What! while I live shall I ever marry thy son?

CREON

There is strong necessity for thee, for by what means wilt thou escape the marriage?

ANTIGONE

That night then shall find me one of the Danaïdæ.

CREON

Dost mark with what audacity she hath insulted us?

ANTIGONE

The steel be witness, and the sword, by which I swear.

CREON

But why art thou so eager to get rid of this marriage?

ANTIGONE

I will take my flight with my most wretched father here.

CREON

There is nobleness in thee; but there is some degree of folly.

ANTIGONE

And I will die with him too, that thou mayest farther know.

CREON

Go—thou shalt not slay my son—quit the land.

ŒDIPUS, ANTIGONE, CHORUS.

ŒDIPUS

O daughter, I praise thee indeed for thy zealous intentions.

ANTIGONE

But if I were to marry, and thou suffer banishment alone, my father?

ŒDIPUS

Stay and be happy; I will bear with content mine own ills.

ANTIGONE

And who will minister to thee, blind as thou art, my father?

ŒDIPUS

Falling wherever it shall be my fate, I will lie on the ground.

ANTIGONE
But Œdipus, where is he? and the renowned Enigmas?

ŒDIPUS
Perished! one day blest me, and one day destroyed.

ANTIGONE
Ought not I then to have a share in thy woes?

ŒDIPUS
To a daughter exile with a blind father is shameful.

ANTIGONE
Not to a right-minded one however, but honorable, my father.

ŒDIPUS
Lead me now onward, that I may touch thy mother.

ANTIGONE
There: touch the aged woman with thy most dear hand.

ŒDIPUS
O mother! Oh most hapless wife!

ANTIGONE
She doth lie miserable, having all ills at once on her.

ŒDIPUS
But where is the fallen body of Eteocles, and of Polynices?

ANTIGONE
They lie extended before thee near one another.

ŒDIPUS
Place my blind hand upon their unhappy faces.

ANTIGONE
There: touch thy dead children with thy hand.

ŒDIPUS
O ye dear wrecks, unhappy, of an unhappy father.

ANTIGONE
O name of Polynices, most dear indeed to me.

ŒDIPUS
Now, my child, is the oracle of Apollo come to pass.

ANTIGONE

What? but dost thou mention evils in addition to these evils?

ŒDIPUS
That I must die an exile at Athens.

ANTIGONE
Where? what citadel of Attica will receive thee?

ŒDIPUS
The sacred Colonus, and the temple of the Equestrian God. But stay—minister to thy blind father here, since thou art desirous of sharing his exile.

ANTIGONE
Go to thy wretched banishment: stretch forth thy dear hand, O aged father, having me as thy guide, as the gale that wafts the ship.

ŒDIPUS
Behold, I go, my child, be thou my unhappy conductor.

ANTIGONE
We are, we are indeed unhappy above all Theban virgins.

ŒDIPUS
Where shall I place my aged footstep? Bring my staff, my child.

ANTIGONE
This way, this way come; here, here place thy foot, thou that hast the strength of a dream.

ŒDIPUS
Alas! alas! for my most wretched flight!—To drive me, old as I am, from my country—Alas! alas! the dreadful, dreadful things that I have suffered!

ANTIGONE
What suffered! what suffered! Vengeance sees not the wicked, nor repays the foolishness of mortals.

ŒDIPUS
That man am I, who mounted aloft to the victorious heavenly song, having solved the dark enigma of the virgin Sphinx.

ANTIGONE
Dost thou bring up again the glory of the Sphinx? Forbear from speaking of thy former successes. These wretched sufferings awaited thee, O father, being an exile from thy country to die any where. Leaving with my dear virgins tears for my loss, I depart far from my country, wandering in state not like a virgin's.

ŒDIPUS
Oh! the excellency of thy mind!

ANTIGONE

In the calamities of a father at least it will make me glorious. Wretched am I, on account of the insults offered to thee and to my brother, who has perished from the family, a corse denied sepulture, unhappy, whom, even if I must die, my father, I will cover with secret earth.

ŒDIPUS
Go, show thyself to thy companions.

ANTIGONE
They have enough of my lamentations.

ŒDIPUS
But make thy supplications at the altars.

ANTIGONE
They have a satiety of my woes.

ŒDIPUS
Go then, where stands the fane of Bacchus unapproached, on the mountains of the Mænades.

ANTIGONE
To whom I formerly, clad in the skin of the Theban fawn, danced the sacred step of Semele on the mountains, conferring a thankless favor on the Gods?

ŒDIPUS
O ye inhabitants of my illustrious country, behold, I, this Œdipus, who alone stayed the violence of the bloodthirsty Sphinx, now, dishonored, forsaken, miserable, am banished from the land. Yet why do I bewail these things, and lament in vain? For the necessity of fate proceeding from the Gods a mortal must endure.

CREON
O greatly glorious Victory, mayest thou uphold my life, and cease not from crowning me!

Euripides – A Short Biography

Euripides is rightly lauded as one of the great dramatists of all time. In his lifetime, he wrote over 90 plays and although only 18 have survived they reveal the scope and reach of his genius.

Euripides is identified with many theatrical innovations that have influenced drama all the way down to modern times, especially in the representation of traditional, mythical heroes as ordinary people in extraordinary circumstances. This new approach led him to pioneer developments that later writers would adapt to comedy. Yet he also became "the most tragic of poets", focusing on the inner lives and motives of his characters in a way previously unknown. He was "the creator of...that cage which is the theatre of Shakespeare's Othello, Racine's Phèdre, of Ibsen and Strindberg," in which "...imprisoned men and women destroy each other by the intensity of their loves and hates", and yet he was also the literary ancestor of comic dramatists as diverse as Menander and George Bernard Shaw.

As would be expected from a life lived 2,500 years ago, details of it are few and far between. Accounts of his life, written down the ages, do exist but whether much is reliable or surmised is open to debate.

Most accounts agree that he was born on Salamis Island around 480 BC, to mother Cleito and father Mnesarchus, a retailer who lived in a village near Athens. Upon the receipt of an oracle saying that his son was fated to win "crowns of victory", Mnesarchus insisted that the boy should train for a career in athletics.

His education was not only confined to athletics: he also studied painting and philosophy under the masters Prodicus and Anaxagoras.

However, what became quickly very clear was that athletics was not to be his way to win crowns of victory. Euripides had been lucky enough to have been born in the era as the other two masters of Greek Tragedy; Sophocles and Æschylus. It was in their footsteps that he was destined to follow.

His first play was performed some thirteen years after the first of Socrates plays and a mere three years after Æschylus had written his classic The Oristria.

Theatre was becoming a very important part of the Greek culture. The Dionysia, held annually, was the most important festival of theatre and second only to the fore-runner of the Olympic games, the Panathenia, held every four years, in its appeal. It was a large festival in ancient Athens in honor of the god Dionysus, the central events of which were the theatrical performances of dramatic tragedies and, from 487 BC, comedies. The Dionysia actually consisted of two related festivals, the Rural Dionysia and the City Dionysia, which took place in different parts of the year.

Euripides first competed in the City Dionysia, in 455 BC, one year after the death of Æschylus, and, incredibly, it was not until 441 BC that he won first prize. His final competition in Athens was in 408 BC. However, The Bacchae and Iphigenia in Aulis were performed after his death in 405 BC and first prize was awarded posthumously. Altogether his plays won first prize only five times.

His plays, and those of Æschylus and Sophocles, indicate a difference in outlook between the three men, most easily explained as a generational gap, although with three great talents overlapping the driving forces may have pushed individual styles onwards perhaps faster than they may otherwise have done. Æschylus still looked back to the archaic period, Sophocles was in transition between periods, and Euripides was fully bonded with the new spirit of the classical age. When Euripides' plays are sequenced in time, they also show a developing pattern:

An early period of high tragedy (Medea, Hippolytus)
A patriotic period at the outset of the Peloponnesian War (Children of Hercules, Suppliants)
A middle period of disillusionment at the senselessness of war (Hecuba, Women of Troy)
An escapist period with a focus on romantic intrigue (Ion, Iphigenia in Tauris, Helen)
A final period of tragic despair (Orestes, Phoenician Women, Bacchae)

However, with over three quarters of his plays lost it is difficult to be certain as to whether the other works would also represent this development (e.g., Iphigenia at Aulis is dated with the 'despairing' Bacchae, yet it contains elements that became typical of New Comedy). In the Bacchae, he restores the chorus and messenger speech to their traditional role in the tragic plot, and the play appears to be the culmination of a regressive or archaizing tendency in his later works.

In one of his earliest surviving plays, Medea, includes a speech that he seems to have written in defence of himself as an intellectual ahead of his time, and to further challenge the times he has put the words in the mouth of the play's heroine:

"If you introduce new, intelligent ideas to fools, you will be thought frivolous, not intelligent. On the other hand, if you do get a reputation for surpassing those who are supposed to be intellectually sophisticated, you will seem to be a thorn in the city's flesh. This is what has happened to me."— Medea.

As we know Athenian tragedies during Euripides' lifetime were a public contest between playwrights. The state funded that contest and awarded prizes to the winners. The language was spoken and sung verse, the performance area included a circular floor or orchestra where the chorus could dance, a space for actors (usually three speaking actors in Euripides' time), a backdrop or skene and some special effects: an ekkyklema (used to bring the skene's "indoors" outdoors) and a mechane (used to lift actors in the air, as in deus ex machina). With the introduction of the third actor (an innovation attributed to Sophocles), acting also began to be regarded as a skill to be rewarded with prizes, requiring a long apprenticeship in the chorus. Euripides and other playwrights accordingly composed more and more arias for accomplished actors to sing and this tendency becomes more marked in his later plays: tragedy for him was a living and ever-changing genre.

Accounts by the famed comic poet, Aristophanes, characterise Euripides as a spokesman for destructive, new ideas, that mirror or help to bring about declining standards in both society and tragedy. However, 5th century tragedy was a social gathering for "carrying out quite publicly the maintenance and development of mental infrastructure" and it offered spectators a "platform for an utterly unique form of institutionalized discussion". A dramatist's role was not just to entertain but also to educate his fellow citizens—he was expected to have a message. Clearly this use of drama to democratize discussion was a very useful tool for all sides. Traditional myth provided the subject matter but the dramatist was meant to be innovative so as to sustain interest, which led to novel characterization of heroic figures and to use the mythical past to talk about present issues. The difference between Euripides and his older colleagues was, again, one of degree: his characters talked about the present more controversially and more pointedly than did those of Æschylus and Sophocles, sometimes even challenging the democratic order. Thus, for example, Odysseus is represented in Hecuba as "agile-minded, sweet-talking, demos-pleasing" i.e., a type of the war-time demagogues that were active in Athens during the Peloponnesian War. His concept is pleasingly simple. He retains the old stories and myths as well as the great names of the past and places them in the lives of contemporary Athenians thereby immediately help the audience understand it from the point of view of their own lives.

As mouthpieces for contemporary issues, they all seem to have had at least an elementary course in public speaking. Sometimes the dialogue often contrasts so strongly with the mythical and heroic setting, it looks as if Euripides aimed at parody, as for example in The Trojan Women, where the heroine's rationalized prayer provokes comment from Menelaus:

Hecuba:....O Zeus, whether you are the Law of Necessity in nature, or the Law of Reason in man, hear my prayers. You are everywhere, pursuing your noiseless path, ordering the affairs of mortals according to justice.

Menelaus: What's this? You are starting a new fashion in prayer.

Athenian citizens were familiar with rhetoric in the assembly and law courts, and some scholars believe that Euripides was more interested in his characters as speakers with cases to argue than as characters with lifelike personalities. They are self-conscious about speaking formally and their rhetoric is shown to be flawed, as if Euripides was exploring the problematical nature of language and communication: "For speech points in three different directions at once, to the speaker, to the person addressed, to the features in the world it describes, and each of these directions can be felt as skewed". Thus in the example above, Hecuba presents herself as a sophisticated intellectual describing a rationalised cosmos yet the speech is ill-matched to her audience, Menelaus (an unsophisticated listener), and soon it is found not to suit the cosmos either (her infant grandson is brutally murdered by the victorious Greeks).

Æschylus and Sophocles were innovative, but Euripides could move easily between tragic, comic, romantic and political effects, a versatility that appears in individual plays and also over the course of his career. Potential for comedy lay in his use of 'contemporary' characters, in his sophisticated tone, his relatively informal Greek, and his ingenious use of plots centered on motifs that later became standard, such as the 'recognition scene'. Other tragedians also used recognition scenes but they were heroic in emphasis, as in Æschylus's The Libation Bearers, which Euripides parodied with his mundane treatment of it in Electra (Euripides was unique among the tragedians in incorporating theatrical criticism in his plays). Traditional myth, with its exotic settings, heroic adventures and epic battles, offered potential for romantic melodrama as well as for political comments on a war theme, so that his plays are an extraordinary mix of elements. The Trojan Women for example is a powerfully disturbing play on the theme of war's horrors, apparently critical of Athenian imperialism (it was composed in the aftermath of the Melian massacre and during the preparations for the Sicilian Expedition) yet it features the comic exchange between Menelaus and Hecuba quoted above and the chorus considers Athens, the "blessed land of Theus", to be a desirable refuge—such complexity and ambiguity are typical both of his "patriotic" and "anti-war" plays.

Tragic poets in the 5th century competed against one another at the City Dionysia, each with a tetralogy consisting of three tragedies and a satyr-play. The few extant fragments of satyr-plays attributed to Æschylus and Sophocles indicate that these were a loosely structured, simple and jovial form of entertainment. However, in Cyclops (the only complete Euripides satyr-play that survives) the entertainment is structured more like a tragedy and introduced a note of critical irony typical of his other work. His genre-bending inventiveness is shown above all in Alcestis, a blend of tragic and satyric elements. This fourth play in his tetralogy for 438 BC (i.e., it occupied the position conventionally reserved for satyr-plays) is a "tragedy" that features Heracles as a satyric hero in conventional satyr-play scenes, involving an arrival, a banquet, a victory over an ogre (in this case, Death), a happy ending, a feast and a departure to new adventures.

Euripides was also a great lyric poet. In Medea, for example, he composed for his city, Athens, "the noblest of her songs of praise". His lyric skills however are not just confined to individual poems: "A play of Euripides is a musical whole....one song echoes motifs from the preceding song, while introducing new ones."

Much of his life and his whole career coincided with the struggle between Athens and Sparta for hegemony in Greece but he didn't live to see the final defeat of his city.

It is said that he died in Macedonia after being attacked by the Molossian hounds of King Archelaus and that his cenotaph near Piraeus was struck by lightning—signs of his unique powers, whether for good or ill. In an account by Plutarch, the complete failure of the Sicilian expedition led Athenians to trade renditions of Euripides' lyrics to their enemies in return for food and drink (Life of Nicias 29). Plutarch is the source also for the story that the victorious Spartan generals, having planned the demolition of Athens and the enslavement of its people, grew merciful after being entertained at a banquet by lyrics from Euripides' play Electra: "they felt that it would be a barbarous act to annihilate a city which produced such men" (Life of Lysander).

In The Frogs, composed after Euripides and Æschylus were both dead, Aristophanes imagines the god Dionysus venturing down to Hades in search of a good poet to bring back to Athens. After a debate between the two deceased bards, the god brings Æschylus back to life as more useful to Athens on account of his wisdom, rejecting Euripides as merely clever. Such comic 'evidence' suggests that Athenians admired Euripides even while they mistrusted his intellectualism, at least during the long war with Sparta.

Euripides had a famous library—one of the first to be privately collected. Although he lived most of his life in the midst of the cultured society of Athens, and was in some respects a leader in it, he grew bitter and despondent over the fierce rivalries and greedy ambitions which ran through the city. He loved the seclusion of his house at Salamis, where it was said that he composed his dramas in a cave.

Euripides fell out of favour with his fellow Athenian citizens and retired to the court of Archelaus, king of Macedon, who treated him with consideration and affection.

At his death, in around 406BC, he was mourned by the king, who, refusing the request of the Athenians that his remains be carried back to the Greek city, buried him with much splendor within his own dominions. His tomb was placed at the confluence of two streams, near Arethusa in Macedonia, and a cenotaph was built to his memory on the road from Athens towards the Piraeus.

Euripides – A Concise Bibliography

Alcestis (438 BC)
Medea (431 BC)
Heracleidae (c. 430 BC)
Hippolytus (428 BC)
Andromache (c. 425 BC)
Hecuba (c. 424 BC)
The Suppliants (c. 423 BC)
Electra (c. 420 BC)
Heracles (c. 416 BC)
The Trojan Women (c. 415 BC)
Iphigenia in Tauris (c. 414 BC)
Ion (c. 414 BC)
Helen (c. 412 BC)
Phoenician Women (c. 410 BC)
Orestes (c.408 BC)
Bacchae (405 BC)
Iphigenia at Aulis (405 BC)
Rhesus
Cyclops

Lost and Fragmentary Plays (Dated)

Peliades (455 BC)
Telephus (438 BC with Alcestis)
Alcmaeon in Psophis (438 BC with Alcestis)
Cretan Women (438 with Alcestis)
Cretans (c. 435 BC)
Philoctetes (431 BC with Medea)
Dictys (431 BC with Medea)
Theristai (satyr play, 431 BC with Medea)
Stheneboea (before 429 BC)
Bellerophon (c. 430 BC)
Cresphontes (ca. 425 BC)
Erechtheus (422 BC)
Phaethon (c. 420 BC)
Wise Melanippe (c. 420 BC)
Alexandros (415 BC with Trojan Women)
Palamedes (415 BC with Trojan Women)
Sisyphus (satyr play, 415 BC with Trojan Women)
Captive Melanippe (c. 412 BC)
Andromeda (412 BC with Helen)
Antiope (c. 410 BC)
Archelaus (c. 410 BC)
Hypsipyle (c. 410 BC)
Alcmaeon in Corinth (c. 405 BC) Won first prize as part of a trilogy with The Bacchae and Iphigenia in Aulis.

Lost and Fragmentary Plays (Not Dated)

Aegeus
Aeolus
Alcmene
Alope, or Cercyon
Antigone
Auge
Autolycus
Busiris
Cadmus
Chrysippus
Danae
Epeius
Eurystheus
Hippolytus Veiled
Ino
Ixion
Lamia
Licymnius
Meleager
Mysians
Oedipus
Oeneus
Oenomaus

Peirithous
Peleus
Phoenix
Phrixus
Pleisthenes
Polyidus
Protesilaus
Reapers
Rhadamanthys
Sciron
Scyrians
Syleus
Temenidae
Temenos
Tennes
Theseus
Thyestes

www.ingramcontent.com/pod-product-compliance
Lightning Source LLC
Chambersburg PA
CBHW060058050426
42448CB00011B/2528